Nigel Farage

In His Own Words

Nigel Farage

In His Own Words

Compiled by
Andrew Liddle

Biteback Publishing

First published in Great Britain in 2015 by
Biteback Publishing Ltd
Westminster Tower
3 Albert Embankment
London SE1 7SP
Copyright in the selection © Andrew Liddle 2015

ISBN 978-1-84954-817-5

10 9 8 7 6 5 4 3 2 1

A CIP catalogue record for this book is available from the British Library.

Set in Futura Std

Printed and bound in Great Britain by
CPI Group (UK) Ltd, Croydon CR0 4YY

CONTENTS

INTRODUCTION

Nigel Farage is one of the most outspoken and controversial politicians ever to grace the British political
stage. Not since Enoch Powell has one man's radical language – and provocative humour – garnered so much
attention and, indeed, derision.

Loved and hated in equal measure, Farage has undoubtedly been the thrust behind the rise of the United Kingdom
Independence Party (UKIP), which is currently on the cusp

of breaking the British political mould. The party's stunning electoral triumph in the 2014 European elections – in which they polled first – would have been impossible without Farage's voracious leadership. And his success has only grown since, with two UKIP MPs now sitting in the House of Commons and a real chance of Farage – and other UKIP candidates – joining them later this year (2015).

Farage has made the party of 'fruitcakes, loonies and closet racists', as David Cameron described them, a household name. And nothing has made him more popular – or, perhaps, well known – than his outspoken antics. Witty, biting, cutting and outrageous, often all at once, Farage has positioned himself as a lone splash of colour in an era of monotone political leaders. He deliberately shuns political correctness, which has led some to reject him as racist and xenophobic, but at least as many to respect him. His words have helped define him as someone who is viewed – despite being a public-school-educated, ex-City trader – as unlike other politicians.

Clad in his trademark Barbour, fag in one hand, pint in the other, Farage has undoubtedly succeeded in making people believe he is like them, and, perhaps even more importantly, speaks for them.

Yet it has not always been this way. Farage – excluding a brief hiatus in 2009 – has been leader of his party since 2006, and, until recently, has hardly electrified the nation. In 2009, UKIP would gain 15 per cent of votes in the European elections – but in 2010 they would receive just over 3 per cent of the vote nationally.

And, despite recent by-election triumphs, the historical precedent for an insurgent party breaking the mould of British politics is patchy at best. The Social Democratic Party (SDP), founded in 1981, won several by-elections and garnered 26 per cent of the vote nationally in 1983, but would actually end up losing seats in our first-past-the-post electoral system. Led by veteran 'big beast' Roy Jenkins – who, apart from smoking and drinking, was little like Farage – the SDP promised a great deal, but ultimately failed to unseat the two main parties from the dinner table of political power.

On the other hand, there is the example of the Scottish National Party in Scotland, who, like UKIP, have focused more on populism than cold policy. From 1992, Alex

Salmond – who is similar to Farage in many ways – began a strategy that would create a dangerous, new and influential force outside the political mainstream. Whether Farage is more of a Salmond than a Jenkins, only time will tell.

Of course, like any modern-day politician, Farage has endured his share of controversy and scandal: an alleged liaison with a 25-year-old Latvian he met in a pub; outrageous expenses claims; and, of course, colourful language on immigration. Comments, for instance, that he felt uncomfortable on a train in which no one in his carriage was speaking English, led to widespread derision in the liberal media, particularly given he is married to a German.

But, as open borders and the free movement of labour have grown into the public consciousness, so Farage has become more popular. He has positioned himself as someone outwith the Westminster cabal – someone who speaks his mind and, some would say, the mind of the British people. Any scandal that he – or more often his party members – are involved in has failed to put the brakes on the UKIP express train.

If anything, they have made him stand out, like a British

Berlusconi. He has appeared in adverts; he has survived cancer, a plane crash and being hit by a car; he is, at the very least, exceptionally lucky.

Anything that hits the Teflon-like Farage, he can inevitably turn into a vote-winner.

Speaking everywhere from the hallowed chambers of the European Parliament to the pubs of middle England, Farage's biting attacks have won him friends and enemies in equal measure. His wicked wit has delighted the growing group of voters disaffected with the UK's three main political parties. His words, as the country approaches the general election later this year, mean that UKIP are posed to potentially deal a deathblow to the Westminster mould.

Whatever their success, there is little doubt that Farage – his words, wisdom and wickedness – have been the central driving force behind the party's meteoric rise.

Never one to shy away from controversy, this book brings together some of the quotes that have made Farage the political phenomenon he is, as well as the responses they have generated. And, in doing so, it provides a snapshot of one man's journey to the pinnacle of political populism.

BIOGRAPHY

Nigel Paul Farage was born on 3 April 1964 in Kent. His father, Guy Oscar Justus Farage, was an alcoholic stockbroker who walked out on the family when Nigel was five years old.

Farage attended the public school Dulwich College. Here he grew to love the classic sports – rugby and cricket – and, one teacher suggests, fascism.

Reaching the age of eighteen, Farage rejected further

education at university, choosing instead to follow in his father's footsteps in a career as a broker in the City. He traded on the metals exchange where he enjoyed the hard-living atmosphere prevalent in the financial services.

After a night in the pub, the young trader was run over by a car. His injuries were so severe doctors thought he might lose a leg. Grainne Hayes, his nurse, would become his first wife. He would go on to have two sons with Ms Hayes – and a further two daughters with his second wife, a German called Kirsten Mehr.

Shortly after recovering from his crash, he was diagnosed with testicular cancer. He came through the experience increasingly determined to make something of his life.

Farage enjoyed moderate success in the City, but his work also helped him develop a more refined political consciousness. A traditional Conservative, he became disillusioned with the party under John Major, particularly after the former premier signed the Maastricht Treaty.

Farage was one of the founding members of the

Anti-Federalist League, which would eventually grow into UKIP. At the 1997 general election, the burgeoning party was overshadowed by the Referendum Party. Despite being backed by multimillionaire businessman Sir James Goldsmith, it soon faded, with UKIP picking up much of its anti-EU support.

In 1999 – and largely thanks to the proportional representation system used at European elections – UKIP made its first breakthrough. Farage was elected to represent the south east of England – one of three UKIP members voted to represent their constituents at the European Parliament.

In 2004, Farage successfully recruited TV presenter and ex-Labour MP Robert Kilroy-Silk to be a candidate in the European elections that year. He was elected – alongside a re-elected Farage and ten other UKIP MEPs – but then attempted to take the party over, before scuttling off to found the short-lived Veritas Party.

In 2006, Farage replaced the less charismatic Roger Knapman as UKIP leader.

Under Farage's helm, the party raised its profile and, in the 2009 European elections, got more votes than

Labour and the Liberal Democrats. That year, Farage also resigned as leader to take on House of Commons Speaker John Bercow in his Buckingham seat.

He crashed an aircraft on election day in 2010 and came third, behind Mr Bercow and a local independent candidate. Farage returned to the leadership of his party later that year.

By the 2013 local elections in England, Farage had raised UKIP's profile to such an extent that it won more than 140 seats and averaged 25 per cent of the vote in the wards where it was standing.

The party would also come second in parliamentary by-elections in Eastleigh and in Wythenshawe and Sale East that year.

In the 2014 European elections, Farage led his party to the top of the poll.

Later that year, he would go head-to-head against Deputy Prime Minister Nick Clegg in two televised debates on Europe.

His party would also gain its first two MPs – Douglas Carswell and Mark Reckless, both Conservative defectors.

Moving into 2015, Farage is poised to play a decisive

role in the May general election, where he is contesting the South Thanet constituency.

NIGEL B.P.
(BEFORE POLITICS)

I never had any intention of being involved in this at all.

Farage discusses his rise to prominence from City trader to political figure

In the 1980s, the City was a great place to be. It was unbelievable. The booze culture was mega. It was competitive. It was quite brutal. It was tough but very exciting. And then there was the money. I was handling millions and drinking more or less continuously. If I'd concentrated on business I would have been a very wealthy man.

Farage on his rather unsuccessful, financially at least, career in the City before he entered politics

VICES

Alastair Campbell: Don't you think we should just say you cannot drink and drive, full stop?

Farage: That would be appalling. I'd have to give up driving!

Farage jokes about his drinking in an interview with Alastair Campbell for *GQ*

BBC reporter: You obviously know Nigel Farage very well and he has got this reputation as a bloke in the saloon bar, but do you think it is telling on him? I mean he works very hard, but perhaps he smokes and drinks too much as well.

Godfrey Bloom: Well, he's never pretended to be a priest...

Godfrey Bloom defends Farage's lifestyle on BBC News. Farage would later go on to disown his old friend after constant erratic behaviour

Alastair Campbell: You project this boozy image of yourself very deliberately.

Farage: That's not fair. You never see pictures of me falling over in the street.

Alastair Campbell: But you do fall over in the street.

Farage: Only when I got hit by a car.

Alastair Campbell, a former alcoholic, talks to Farage about his drinking in an interview for *GQ*

He doesn't get a lot of sleep, he doesn't get a lot of rest, he lives on adrenalin a lot, he doesn't eat regular meals – now I am beginning to sound like his mother – and he smokes and he drinks too much.

But if you have that sort of lifestyle I think it is what keeps him going, it keeps the adrenalin going.

Kirsten Farage, who works as Mr Farage's taxpayer-funded secretary, admits in an interview with the *Daily Telegraph* that she worries about her husband's lifestyle, which is part-and-parcel of his popularity

I'll tell you something: I work an eighteen-hour day most days and I think I'm entitled at lunchtime to a pint.

Farage justifies his drinking

Actually, he is a *bon viveur*. His wife is a European continental. He is an expert on the finest European red wines. He is very different in private – we sat with him after *Question Time* and he went through the wine list with the maître d' with the aplomb of a man who has spent years in the European Parliament…

George Galloway describes Farage after their meeting on *Question Time*

Never. I think at eighteen I took the view that I am already drinking and smoking, so I'll draw the line there.

In an interview with Alastair Campbell, published in *GQ*, Farage said he had never taken drugs – because at eighteen he was already smoking and drinking. He also, in the same interview, admitted to smoking two packs of cigarettes a day while in hospital recovering from being hit by a car

Of course, the great danger with young people is if you ban things it makes them more attractive.

Obesity is killing more people than smoking, you could ban chip shops, you could ban doughnuts. The point is we are big enough and ugly enough to make our own decisions.

Farage discusses UKIP plans to reverse the smoking ban, which he branded 'silly and illiberal'

As I'm sure many people realise, I am quite a keen smoker. I've always prized myself on being rather good at it.

Farage writes on smoking for a column in *The Independent*

I have to say, as a smoker, frankly I haven't yet given up but I could do very easily.

Farage speaks on giving up smoking during a ninety-second video promoting e-cigarette use as a method of kicking the habit

I think it is all utterly bloody barmy.

Sometimes for a bit of fun I have asked for defunct brands like Capstan Full Strength, Craven A Lights and, when they can't find them, I ask for the manager.

It is just nuts, it's bonkers.

Farage speaks to the *Asian Trader* magazine on his irritation with having cigarette packets behind shutters in larger shops

IMMIGRATION

Give us our country back.

Farage issues a rallying cry to party members in 2013

What we've done is say to 485 million people: 'You can all come, every one of you. You're unemployed? You've got a criminal record? Please come. You've got nineteen children? Please come.' We've lost any sense of perspective on this.

Farage's views on immigration have drawn international interest, such as these comments made to the *Washington Post*

We have literally made this country now the cheap labour economy of the European Union.

Farage tells a UKIP hustings in Rochester that immigration has radically changed the UK labour market

If you said to me, 'do you want to see another five million people come to Britain, and if that happened we would all be slightly richer,' I would say, 'do you know what, I would rather we were not slightly richer.'

Farage addresses arguments that immigration brings economic growth on BBC Radio 4's *Today* programme

Newsweek Europe: So quality means people without a homicide conviction?

Farage: Yes. And people who do not have HIV, to be frank. That's a good start. And people with a skill.

Farage appears to suggest that those with HIV should be denied entry to the UK in an interview with *Newsweek Europe*. He later added that TB cases from Eastern Europe were costing the NHS 'a great deal of money'

The National Health Service is for British people and for families who have paid into this system for generations.

Farage describes his vision of the NHS

To have a total policy solution after the disaster that has engulfed us since Labour came to power in 1997 is no easy matter.

Farage discusses his proposed five-year immigration ban on BBC Radio 4's *Today* programme

I'm not giving you the *Love, Actually* version of what makes Britain different.

Farage shows his knowledge of popular culture while describing his views on the UK

James O'Brien: What about if a group of German children [moved in]? What's the difference?

Farage: You know what the difference is … We want an immigration system based on controlling not only quantity but quality as well.

Farage has a heated interview with LBC's James O'Brien. The pair clashed over the differences between immigrants from various countries

When Dermot Murnaghan read a quotation to Nigel Farage about the effects of immigration on 'indigenous' Britons, the UKIP leader agreed with it, only to be told that the words came from Enoch Powell's infamous 'Rivers of Blood' speech. Undaunted, he endorsed Powell's 'basic principle'. Indeed Farage remembers even as a school boy giving 'spirited defences' of a man who called for the repatriation of non-white people.

The Guardian's Leo Benedictus on Farage

In scores of our cities and market towns, this country, in a short space of time, has frankly become unrecognisable.

Farage on immigration at conference in Torquay

It was a stopper going out and we stopped at London Bridge, New Cross, Hither Green; it was not until we got past Grove Park that I could hear English being audibly spoken in the carriage. Does that make me feel slightly awkward? Yes it does.

Farage cited an experience on a rush-hour train leaving Charing Cross as one of the justifications for his comments on immigration

I'm not saying people on trains should be forced to speak English. That's a bloody stupid question.

Farage fields questions on his Charing Cross train example of problem immigration

James O'Brien: You felt uncomfortable about people speaking foreign languages despite the fact that presumably your own wife does when she phones home to Germany.

Farage: I don't suppose she speaks it on the train.

Farage struggles to defend his train analogy in an interview with LBC

If the eurozone goes as badly over the next few years as I still believe that it will, we face the prospect of the largest migratory wave that has ever come to this country and we have three political parties who are not prepared to do anything about it.

Farage claims it is not just Eastern European immigration that concerns him

I do not wish for people to feel in a discriminatory manner towards Romanians but I do say there is a very real problem here that everybody else has brushed under the carpet – the whole organised crime element and the impact that has had on London and other parts of the country. That is a serious issue.

Farage urges caution on Romanian immigration

I think the mask is starting to slip and I think what's being revealed [is] that sort of behind the beer-swilling bonhomie is a rather nasty view of the world.

Nick Clegg responds to Farage's comments on Romanian immigrants on BBC One's *The Andrew Marr Show*

[Immigration is] the biggest single issue facing this country. It affects the economy, the NHS, schools, public services, the deficit. But the establishment has been closing down the immigration debate for twenty years. UKIP has opened it up.

Farage highlights how UKIP's stance on immigration has won it considerable popularity among voters

RELIGION

I approve of Jesus. He seems a decent sort who liked his wine and the company of riff-raff.

Farage on God

A lot of this is our own fault. We have been too weak. My country is a Judeo-Christian country. So we've got to actually start standing up for our values.

Farage believes the decline of traditional values is responsible for Islamic radicalisation in much of the UK

I'm getting a bit tired of my kids coming home from school being taught about every other religion in the world, celebrating every other religious holiday, but not actually being taught about Christianity.

Farage discusses multiculturalism in British schools

I have to say this: if you really think that taking on fundamentalist radical Islam in battle is something that we can somehow succeed in, I suspect we will launch ourselves, in the same way we have in Afghanistan, on a decade of unending, unwinnable misery. I do not want the United Kingdom to be part of a militaristic, warlike European Union.

Farage describes his anti-interventionist stance in the European Parliament

In the war against Islamic extremism, Vladimir Putin, whatever we may think of him as a human being, is actually on our side.

Farage has regularly praised Russian President Vladimir Putin, including in the European Parliament as quoted here

I have to say that when I listened to Tony Blair, with Tory support, in 2003, arguing that if we invaded Iraq it would make the streets of Britain safer, I didn't believe it at the time. But even I've been surprised by the extent to which many in the Muslim community have seen what America and Britain have done as an attack on them and an attack on their values.

While radicalisation is not a purely British thing, I think we have made it very much worse.

Farage speaking about ISIS on *Channel 4 News*, 21 August 2014

THE EUROPEAN
PARLIAMENT

I want you all fired.

Farage to members of the European Parliament

I've been in the European Parliament for fifteen years and I have never once voted.

Farage on his voting record in the European Parliament

My voters did not vote for me to go native. They didn't vote for me to move to Brussels, they voted for me to campaign to get out of the European Union and that's what I'm going to go on doing.

Farage, using a colonial anachronism, defends his voting record in the European Parliament

On the plus side, Mr Juncker, you are a sociable cove, with a very much better sense of humour than most people I've met in Brussels ... but we are being asked to vote for the ultimate Brussels insider: somebody who has always operated with dark backroom deals and stitch-ups.

Farage puts politics ahead of personal affability and slams Jean-Claude Juncker as the nominee for President of the European Commission

We are all going to be asked to vote – and we have got one candidate to vote for! It is like good old Soviet times, isn't it?

Farage on the election of Jean-Claude Juncker as President of the European Commission

You would have thought: when in a hole, stop digging. But no, Dave [David Cameron] kept on digging away. And, I must say, as the final vote approached it began to feel a bit like the Eurovision Song Contest, where it doesn't really matter how good the British entry is: such is the dislike of our country around much of Europe, we're always going to lose.

Farage compares Cameron's attempts to stop Juncker becoming European Commission President to the Eurovision Song Contest, which the UK last won in 1997

Mr Farage, what are you doing here? What I heard is the speech of the opposition in the House of Commons. If you want to hold that kind of speech, get elected there. What are you doing here?

Philippe Lamberts MEP, leader of the Green group, attacks Farage following his speech criticising Jean-Claude Juncker

This isn't the first time on leaving my island that I have had difficulty with the microphones in Europe, because, in the European Parliament, President Schulz can't wait to turn my microphone off, so I'm fairly used to this sort of thing.

Farage entertains the Campaign for a Neutral and Independent Switzerland during technical difficulties

How can somebody like Prince Charles be allowed to come to the European Parliament at this time and announce he thinks it should have more powers? It would have been better for the country he wants to rule one day if he had stayed home and tried to persuade Gordon Brown to give people the promised referendum on the Treaty of Lisbon.

Farage remained firmly in his seat while Prince Charles received a standing ovation from hundreds of British MEPs after he made a speech in the European Parliament on climate change

It reminded me of young Mr Grace in that old TV series *Are You Being Served?*

Farage on Prince Charles's speech to the European Parliament

I was embarrassed and disgusted when the leader of the UK Independence Party, Nigel Farage, remained firmly seated during the lengthy standing ovation Prince Charles received. I had not realised Mr Farage's blind adherence to right-wing politics involved disloyalty and discourtesy to the royal family. He should be thoroughly ashamed of himself and should apologise to the British people he represents.

Farage strikes a nerve with Gary Titley, former leader of the European Parliamentary Labour Party

Greece is being driven into the ground, and I think, frankly, when it comes to chaos, you ain't seen nothing yet!

Farage speaks in the European Parliament in Strasbourg on the debt meltdown in Greece that caused significant rioting and civil disobedience

[You said] when we had a president, we'd see a giant global political figure.

The man that would be the political leader for 500 million people – the man that would represent all of us on the world stage. The man whose job is so important that, of course, you are paid more than President Obama.

Well, I'm afraid what we got was you. And I'm sorry, but after that performance earlier that you gave – and I don't want to be rude, but you know – you have the charisma of a damp rag and the appearance of a low-grade bank clerk.

And the question that I want to ask is: who are you? I'd never heard of you – nobody in Europe had ever heard of you.

Farage to the first President of the European Council, Herman Van Rompuy

Martin Schulz: It is not acceptable that, in this Parliament, a group chairman not only criticises a President of the Council but calls him a wet rag.

Farage: You may not like what I say, but just consider your behaviour. You, after the Irish people in a referendum voted no, said that our group – by supporting a no vote – had opened the door to fascism. You said that we had behaved as a group in the Parliament like Hitler and the Nazis in the Reichstag.

Farage at the European Parliament debate with Martin Schulz on the appointment of Herman Van Rompuy as President of the Council

I've decided that I will make an apology. The only people I'm going to apologise to are bank clerks the world over. And, if I have offended them, I'm very sorry indeed.

Farage's semi-apology following his Herman Van Rompuy attacks

His behaviour towards Mr Rompuy was inappropriate, unparliamentary and insulting to the dignity of the House.

Jerzy Buzek speaks after Farage was fined for refusing to apologise to Van Rompuy

'What does being so rude achieve?'

'Well, it has got me on this programme, hasn't it?'

Farage defends his description of Herman Van Rompuy on BBC Radio 4's *Today* programme

This budget deal is game, set and match to President Chirac: no cheese-eating surrender monkeys. He, unlike you, stands up for the French national interests.

Farage attacks British Prime Minister Tony Blair during a session in 2005 at the European Parliament, when the former Labour leader was President of the European Council

Let me tell you, sir: you sit with our country's flag – you do not represent our country's interest. This is the year 2005 – not 1945. We are not fighting each other anymore: these are our partners, these are our colleagues and our future lies in Europe.

Tony Blair's response to Farage, European Parliament committee

José Manuel Barroso: I was elected by this Parliament, by a secret vote, so I think I deserve the respect of this Parliament – from all members.

Farage: Well, Mr Barroso, I enjoyed that enormously. The fact that you can stand up and boast about the fact that you were elected in secret and that that somehow this gives you democratic legitimacy is the most bizarre concept I have come across in my entire life.

Farage's exchange with José Manuel Barroso, European Parliament

What you didn't tell us in your speech was about the fact that you actually know Mr Gaddafi. Indeed, you went to meet him in December, didn't you? Do you remember?

There's a jolly nice photograph of you and Mr Gaddafi holding hands. In fact, I have to say, I've never seen you smiling more or looking happier.

Farage to Herman Van Rompuy during Libya mission

President Hollande, despite your own views, you are doing rather a lot for the Eurosceptic debate in France. The decision to reduce the retirement age, increase the minimum wage, but, above all, of course, the hate tax – to make sure that all your successful entrepreneurs and now footballers are fleeing France – all means that the competitiveness gap between Germany and France is getting wider.

Farage, speaking in the European Parliament, slams Hollande's more left-wing policies

Coming from the UK, we didn't even realise that these elections were seen to be significant, as far as the next Commission President was concerned.

The Tories didn't have a horse in the race, the British Labour Party disowned Martin Schulz. And the Liberal Democrats, who I'm pleased to say collapsed to one member – had they put old Verhofstadt on the television, they would have lost the lot.

Nigel Farage addresses the European Parliament in Strasbourg following UKIP's remarkable electoral triumph in the 2014 European elections

LEADERS

Nice chap. Not very worldly. I would love to see him in a working men's club in Newcastle.

Farage on Labour Party leader Ed Miliband

Cameron is a perfectly nice fellow who stands foursquare for nothing.

Farage on Conservative Party leader David Cameron

Well, I know him best because we worked together in the European Parliament. Very nice guy, just wrong.

Farage on Liberal Democrat leader Nick Clegg

The guy is a deluded idiot.

Farage on President Obama

When I went for Nicolas Sarkozy, he loved it and I subsequently got invited to a lunch at the Élysée Palace. Can't turn that down – me and an array of ghastly people. Wonderful lunch. Sarko got out these Romeo cigars – to everyone's disgust – and he and I had a jolly good smoke.

Farage describes how his attack on Nicolas Sarkozy was well received by the former French President

When you meet Angela Merkel in private, she looks even more miserable than she does in public.

Farage speaks to a UKIP meeting in 2012 about German Chancellor Angela Merkel

He's the only Tory politician who UKIP members listen to and agree with much of what he says.

Farage on Boris Johnson

I personally hold a grudge against Silvio Berlusconi. He didn't invite me to his leaving party and I'm greatly aggrieved by that.

Farage jokes with UKIP members at a meeting in 2012, playing on Berlusconi's reputation as something of a party animal

But there's certainly only one thing I could never agree with George Galloway on. He's a teetotaller and wants to close all the bars in the House of Commons. That is just not on.

Farage discusses the similarities – and differences – between himself and 'Gorgeous George'

You made it clear that Cameron was wrong, he was deceiving the British people, and you made it clear that you were the boss, and not him, and for that, I thank you and wish you a very happy retirement indeed.

Farage gives tongue-in-cheek praise to José Manuel Barroso on his retirement as head of the European Commission

I remember your first big act as Chancellor, when you sold 400 metric tons of gold on the world's exchanges at $275 an ounce. At today's valuation, that would be $10 billion dollars higher. But it isn't just the fact you got it wrong, because we can all get it wrong. It is the fact that you announced in advance how much you were going to sell and on what day you were going to sell it. It was an error so basic that the average A-level economics student, even in these educationally devalued times, would not have done it.

We haven't heard an apology. Your government has apologised for the Amritsar massacre, you have apologised for slavery, you have apologised for virtually everything. Will you please apologise for what you did as British Chancellor and then perhaps we might just listen to you.

To Gordon Brown in the European Parliament

She's never had a proper job and she's never been elected to anything in her life, so I guess she's perfect for this European Union.

Farage on the selection of Cathy Ashton as the EU's High Representative for Foreign Affairs

The Lib Dems still think that the euro is a success! I don't quite know where Cleggy gets this from. I don't know, perhaps he is considering an alternative career as a stand-up comedian once he's out of politics.

Farage mocks Nick Clegg for his views on the euro at a UKIP meeting in 2012

I nearly choked on my bacon roll when I heard Nick Clegg say he wanted to have a debate.

Farage describes his surprise at the Deputy Prime Minister's decision to accept a debate on the EU with him

Clegg's European at heart, not British.

Farage on the Deputy Prime Minister before their head-to-head debate

The alternative of President Kinnock is too awful.

Farage articulates his views on the monarchy in Britain

And you come here, Mr Samaras, and tell us that you represent the 'sovereign will of the Greek people'. Well, I am sorry, but you are not in charge of Greece, and I suggest you rename and rebrand your party. It is called 'New Democracy'; I suggest you call it 'No Democracy' because Greece is now under foreign control.

Farage attacks Greek Prime Minister Antonis Samaras in the European Parliament in Strasbourg

@Nigel_Farage: I met Pope Francis this morning in Strasbourg.

Farage seems casually dismissive on Twitter after meeting the Pontiff

If this was supposed to be the speech that turned the tide of Cameron's fortunes he may well wish he had never made it.

Reacting to David Cameron's long-awaited speech on immigration

Maybe this will be the beginning of a trend? Flat taxes, cutting foreign aid, a referendum on Europe, grammar schools. Who knows?

Farage hopes for more plagiarism from the Conservative Party after Theresa May was caught out for repeating an anecdote of the UKIP leader's in her 2011 conference speech

THE EU

I think we should just tell them to get stuffed, frankly.

Farage on demands from the EU for an approximate €2 billion increase in the UK's rebate

It is a European Union of economic failure, of mass unemployment and of low growth.

Farage on the state of the EU

When people stand up and talk about the great success that the EU has been, I'm not sure anybody saying it really believes it themselves anymore.

Farage on his perceived decline of the EU

We seek an amicable divorce from the European Union and its replacement with a genuine free-trade agreement, which is what my parents' generation thought we had signed up for in the first place.

Farage on leaving the EU

The euro *Titanic* has now hit the iceberg – and there simply aren't enough lifeboats to go round.

Farage on the eurozone crisis

We pay £53 million a day to be a member of this organisation for no benefit whatsoever. Mr Cameron, when you come back from this Brussels summit, why don't you accept my challenge and let us have a proper full debate on Britain and whether it's worth staying as member of this Union or not?

The last opinion polls over the weekend show that now, by a majority of two to one, the British people want us to leave this Union and not to pay you a penny piece.

Farage at the European Parliament

Increasingly people are saying: we don't want that flag, we don't want the anthem, we don't want this political class – we want the whole thing consigned to the dustbin of history.

Farage at the European Parliament

We had the French say 'no', we had the Dutch say 'no' – and then we had the Irish say 'no'. And this Parliament has wilfully carried on, ignoring the wishes of the people. You just don't get it, do you? No means no.

Farage gets passionate after France and Holland reject the European Constitution. It was still introduced as part of the Lisbon Treaty, despite the 'no' votes

You are nationalistic, you are bullying, you are threatening, you are anti-democratic – you are a complete shower.

Nigel Farage after 'no' votes in referenda to EU Constitution

Angela Merkel: I can't imagine that the UK would not be part of Europe and I think it is good, also, for the UK to be part of Europe. If you have a world of seven billion and you are alone in that world I don't think that is good for the UK. And so I will do everything to keep the UK in the European Union as a good partner.

Farage: Wouldn't it be better, Chancellor, if you went tonight to Downing Street and said to Mr Cameron, look: this simply doesn't work anymore, it really is time that the United Kingdom left the European Union? He hasn't got the courage to say it himself but, if you said it to him, it might have an impact.

All I'm suggesting, Chancellor, is that we have a simple, amicable divorce and then we'll all get on much better in the future.

Farage and Angela Merkel debate at the European Parliament

On the basis that your Employment Minister says the country is bankrupt, what do you do? Well, the old trick, launch a foreign military intervention.

So your troops go off to Mali and, yes, it is very good to see the smiling faces in Timbuktu for the moment, but you've done this on behalf of the European Union. It is now an EU mission. Just two days ago, Tony Blair said the European Union is not about peace, the European Union is about power.

I think what he meant is that the European Union, increasingly, will be about war.

Farage attacks Hollande over dragging the EU into the peacekeeping mission in Mali

We wouldn't want to be like the Swiss, would we? That would be awful! We'd be rich!

Farage gives a running commentary on Cameron's 2013 speech promising an in/out referendum on the EU if the Conservatives get a majority at the 2015 general election later this year

I have become used to the Tory Party mimicking our policies and phrases in a desperate effort to pretend to their members they are still Eurosceptic.

Farage on the Conservative Party

Mr Cameron, you have my phone number.

Farage has repeatedly demanded that the Prime Minister debate him on Britain's place in the EU

It's the career political class and their friends in big business, they want us to keep this status quo and I want Britain to get up off its knees; let's govern ourselves again, stand tall and trade with the world.

The end of Farage's introductory statement in his debate on Britain and the EU with Nick Clegg. Farage believes the two debates had a substantial impact on UKIP's success in the 2014 European elections

I'd do a deal with the devil if he got me what I wanted.

Farage hints that he might do a deal with Labour in an interview with the *New Statesman*'s editor Jason Cowley

That's the first time I ever received such applause and I am tempted, Mr Verhofstadt, I am tempted to sit down, but – if I may – sadly, the story continues.

Farage responds to sarcastic applause from pro-EU MEPs as he tells his version of recent European history

You said in your speech that none but those on the extremes oppose the European Union. Well, that may be right among professional, career politicians, but a clear majority of the British people want us to have friendship and free trade with the Europe Union – but do not want us to be members of this political union.

To Gordon Brown in the European Parliament

When we launched our party, just 17 per cent of British people agreed we should withdraw from the European Union. Today, that figure is 67 per cent.

Farage describes the growing antipathy among people in Britain to the European Union

I'm Nigel Farage – and I love Europe. No, I really do. The wine, the food, the excellent transport systems, the clogs – and the greatest golfers in the world.

Farage stars in a Paddy Power advert promoting the Ryder Cup

I found the Pope's speech remarkable and personally very encouraging, for he implied that the modern European Union had gone badly wrong and the idea of a united European state wasn't even desirable, never mind necessary.

Farage attempts to find an ally in Pope Francis, following the Pontiff's speech to the European Parliament in 2014

Right now the Constitution is mere paper, with no bearing upon the British people, although they might find it good for doorstops, good for real fires and good for fish and chips.

Farage on the European Constitution

No longer do we wish to pay money to Hungarian companies involved in projects that improve the lifestyle and living standards of dogs. And our patience has completely snapped at such cultural absurdities as the 400,000 euros given to the flying gorillas' dance troupe, who are using their own language of rhythm, music and gibberish – well, they'd fit in well here, wouldn't they? – to give performances such as the brilliant smelly-foot dance, with an acoustic score that includes some spectacular belching.

No, I am not making it up.

Nigel Farage at the European Parliament

RACISM

I think that politics needs a bit of spicing up.

Farage's verdict after an advert featuring Rik Mayall as Hitler shouting *'Ein Volk! Ein Reich! Ein Euro!'* ('One people! One empire! One euro!') caused considerable controversy in 2002

**David Emms: It was naughtiness, not racism …
I didn't probe too closely into that naughtiness,
but the staff were fed up with his cheekiness and
rudeness … They wanted me to expel him, but I
saw his potential, made him a prefect, and I was
proved right.**

Former Master of Dulwich College David Emms discusses the issues surrounding making Farage a prefect when he attended the school. Channel 4 published a letter from former teacher Chloe Deakin to Emms in which Farage is described as 'neo-fascist' and 'racist'

Do most fair-minded people think that about us? No. Was some of the media a misrepresentation of us in the run-up to the European election? Yes, it was, and some of it was utterly monstrous.

Farage dismisses allegations that UKIP is a racist party

When Nick Robinson interviewed me at that launch of our campaign I am treated like a Serbian war criminal.

Farage slams his treatment by the BBC's political editor at the launch of their 2014 European election campaign

Nigel Farage is not racist but his comments are deeply offensive.

Labour leader Ed Miliband on Farage

THE RISE OF UKIP

Reporter: Four words: Liberal Democrats, Nick Clegg.

Farage: Goodbyeeeeeeeeeeeeeeee!

Farage speaks after UKIP top the poll in the 2014 Euro elections. The Liberal Democrats kept just one MEP in that election

[It is] the best night in UKIP's history.

Farage speaks following the victory of Douglas Carswell in the Clacton by-election

We're after you – you have underestimated us.

Farage warns Labour and the Conservatives that their two-party hegemony is no longer invincible following UKIP's Clacton by-election victory

One thing many have in common: they are fed up to the back teeth with the cardboard cut-out careerists in Westminster.

The spot-the-difference politicians.

Desperate to fight the middle ground, but can't even find it.

Focus groupies.

The triangulators.

The dog whistlers.

The politicians who daren't say what they really mean.

And that's why UKIP attracts this eclectic support.

Farage describes what attracts voters to UKIP in his 2013 conference speech

We are changing the face of British politics.

Farage in his 2013 UKIP conference speech

We're targeting everyone.

Farage believes that UKIP's appeal can stretch beyond just disaffected Tory voters

Better to be one-man band than no-man band.

Farage responds to the suggestion that UKIP would be nowhere without him

We've thirty thousand members and growing fast. Certainly, by the time of the general election, we'll be the third-highest membership party in Britain. Every other party is fighting their decline.

While some of Farage's predictions from his 2013 conference speech have been proved correct, the Scottish National Party, following the 'no' vote in 2014, is now the third-biggest party in Britain

I am delighted at Des's support in these elections. And I thank him for his rewrite of the lyrics of 'Send in the Clowns' which we are planning to sing at our South East conference.

Farage welcomes the support of famed sports journalist Des Lynam who revealed he would be voting UKIP in 2013

The day after Douglas Carswell joined UKIP we were told Britain had been put on a heightened state of emergency, so listeners can make their own minds up.

Farage claims that Cameron raised the terror threat level in 2014 as a distraction from Tory defections to UKIP

There are two types of people in politics: those who want to be something and those who want to do something.

Farage on UKIP's aim to change the nature of debate in British politics

Have you met the cretins we have in Westminster? Do you think we can be worse than that?

Farage to journalist Richard Godwin

I'm jolly well going to make sure that in the European election of next year many more of you despise me, UKIP and the many millions that are going to vote for us.

Farage on accepting his Insurgent of the Year Award at *The Spectator*'s Parliamentarian of the Year Awards

You can't put a cigarette paper between them on policy.

Farage uses a smoking analogy to describe the differences – or lack thereof – between the three main British political parties

There will be MPs who will work out actually they've got a better chance standing as UKIP. If they join us, I'll be delighted. If they don't, frankly that doesn't really matter.

Farage throws down the gauntlet on BBC Radio 4's *Today* programme after Mark Reckless's victory in the Rochester by-election for UKIP

Even before these results, I saw big representatives of the so-called three main parties – perhaps we'll call them legacy parties from hereafter – and they were on telly and they all looked like goldfish that had just been tipped out of the bowl onto the floor – gasping for air, desperate for something to say.

Farage speaks after UKIP top the poll in the 2014 Euro elections

I believe that the ability to talk to people, and have them feeling engaged rather than patronised, isn't something you can learn. It's a bit like being able to sing or play cricket. You can either do it, or you can't.

Farage on his ability to communicate with a wide audience

We want to signal to everyone we are now parking our tanks on the Labour Party's lawn.

Farage uses a military analogy to illustrate UKIP's strategy of targeting Labour voters as much as Conservative voters

The deracinated political elite of parasites, the bureaucrats, the Eurocrats, the quangocrats, the expenses-fiddlers, the assorted chancers, living it up at taxpayers' expense

It is UKIP's role to sweep them all away, Farage believes

- **Douglas Carswell – brave October**

- **Whatever policies – immigration no. 1 issue**

- **VOTE UKIP GET UKIP**

Some notes recovered from Farage's 2014 Doncaster conference speech

I never thought I would say that the biggest boost that was given to me and UKIP was thanks to Nick Clegg.

Farage cites his two televised debates on the future of the UK in the EU with the Deputy Prime Minister as being crucial to UKIP's recent electoral success

The Clacton by-election is of huge significance not just to the future of UKIP but to the whole of British politics. It will indeed be our high noon.

Farage on the importance of the Clacton by-election

WOMEN

Maybe it is because I've got so many women pregnant over the years that I have a different view.

Farage explains his views on maternity leave

I can't change biology.

Farage responds to comments he made that women who choose to have children will be 'worth far less' to their employer when they come back because their client base cannot be stuck rigidly to them

Farage chuckles at the idea that he does not like women. In 2006 he drunkenly suspended his hostility to the EU's open borders policy to accept an invitation for a late-night drink from a 'sleek and seductive' 25-year-old Latvian called Lita.

Lita told the *News of the World* that Farage was something of a stud and that they had had sex seven times before he fell asleep, 'snoring like a horse'.

George Parker in the *FT* magazine

I think that particular comment was a joke – I have found nothing in this guy's background to suggest he is a political extremist at all.

Farage responds to a comment from Robert Iwaszkiewicz, a Polish MEP who joined Farage's EFD group, who claimed that beating women 'helps bring wives back to Earth'

THE WORDS
OF OTHERS

A rather engaging geezer. He's anti-pomposity, he's anti-political correctness, he's anti-loony Brussels regulation. He's in favour of low tax, sticking up for small business and sticking up for Britain. We Tories look at him, with his pint and cigar and sense of humour, and instinctively recognise someone fundamentally indistinguishable from us.

Boris Johnson on Farage

He looks like a frog who has long ago given up hope of being kissed by a princess, and doesn't much mind.

Peter Hitchens gives his version of Farage in a piece for the *American Spectator*

I always think he looks like somebody has put their finger up his bottom and he really rather likes it.

Conservative MP Anna Soubry on Farage

Farage is a heavy consumer of Rothmans cigarettes and enjoys sea-fishing and country sports. A Barbour-clad Farage loves cricket and used to be seen enjoying hare coursing – until it was banned in 2005. In short he is a youngish fogey: most people are surprised to learn he is still in his forties.

George Parker describes Farage in the *FT* magazine

I remember the first time I interviewed Mr Farage, years ago, before he had anything like a national presence. I asked him how to pronounce his name.

'What do you put your car in?' he asked me.

'Well, I put my car in a garage,' I retorted, pronouncing the last syllable to rhyme with what UKIP housewives are supposed to clean behind. He looked rather crestfallen.

Cathy Newman, Channel 4 presenter, on her first interview with Farage. He also used the same line with BBC presenter Jeremy Paxman

I have had Mr Watson accuse me of behaving like an English football hooligan just because I pointed out that Commissioner Barrot was a convicted embezzler. Gary Titley said that apparently I am a paranoid reactionary living on the fringes of society. Well, I mean he may have a point, I don't know.

Farage gets excited about his political opponents' descriptions of him

He said fruitcakes and loonies. And he said worse than that – he said extremists.

Farage responds to David Cameron's infamous description of UKIP members on *Have I Got News for You*. The panel would later play a game of 'Fruitcake or Loony' in which Farage correctly guessed that his party treasurer and biggest donor, Stuart Wheeler, was a 'fruitcake'

@Nigel_Farage: It's rare to find someone so honest in media, particularly in comedy. This is very interesting.

@frankieboyle: There are a lot of honest people in comedy, which is why they keep calling you a cunt.

@Nigel_Farage: Probably the funniest thing I've heard you say!

@frankieboyle: You didn't hear me say it you daft bastard.

Farage and comedian Frankie Boyle engage in a Twitter spat following Farage's posting of a piece by funnyman Andrew Lawrence slamming stand-up comics who attack UKIP

Mr Farage said new policies would be 'similar in flavour' to his past manifesto pledges, which included bringing in a dress code for taxi drivers, repainting trains to traditional colours and introducing a dress code for taxi drivers.

Georgia Graham, *Daily Telegraph*

Sir, following your articles about UKIP, I would like to make clear that I am as partial to crumpet as the next man, just not as much as Farage.

Godfrey Bloom in a letter to *The Times*

GAFFES

You can't blame me for everything.

As UKIP's popularity has grown, so too has media scrutiny of it. Farage, as in this case, has often had to defend or distance himself from local party members who have been caught in numerous embarrassing positions

I would like to know a bit more about the circumstances. Hitting Michael Crick over the head – tempting, I can understand that, but I wouldn't do it.

[Calling a group of women sluts] sounds appalling, it sounds wholly and highly inappropriate. Clearly, it was his attempt at a joke. It sounds very, very stupid.

Farage responds to former UKIP MEP Godfrey Bloom branding women 'sluts' before hitting Channel 4 reporter Michael Crick with a party manifesto

How we can possibly be giving £1 billion a month, when we're in this sort of debt, to Bongo Bongo Land is completely beyond me. To buy Ray-Ban sunglasses, apartments in Paris, Ferraris and all the rest of it that goes with most of the foreign aid.

Farage forced Godfrey Bloom to promise never to use the phrase 'Bongo Bongo Land' after it garnered significant controversy

And now for the weather for all areas of the British Isles, but definitely not Bongo Bongo Land.

Farage produced a spoof weather forecast on the BBC's *Sunday Politics* after a number of his members – including MEP Godfrey Bloom – were involved in political gaffes. In the segment, he points to the strange conduct of a number of local members from other political parties

Had he done this in any other context than UKIP, there wouldn't be a row at all. But because it's UKIP people will scream blue murder.

And I tell you what gets me. We've had more condemnation and outrage from left-wing commentators about Mike Read's 'Calypso' than we've had over the grooming and rape of thousands of young girls in the north of England.

Farage defends 'UKIP Calypso' song on LBC radio. The song, by radio DJ Mike Read, was sung in a Jamaican accent, causing controversy

I should not have bought the policy ... It was an error.

Farage apologises after it emerged in 2013 that he had established an off-shore trust fund in the Isle of Man, a tax haven. The Farage Family Education Trust 1654 was set up with the intention of limiting the amount of inheritance tax Farage's children would have to pay

Dear old Godders...

Farage responds to Godfrey Bloom MEP claiming 'no employer with a brain in the right place would employ a young, single, free woman'

Enough is enough, let people tell their jokes. If what they say is inappropriate they won't earn a living because they won't get booked again.

Farage responds to *Sunday Mirror* reports that comedian Paul Eastwood made inappropriate jokes at a black-tie dinner held after the UKIP conference in Torquay

Mr Schulz regularly calls people fascists and, when he is called one, the member in question is asked to leave. That isn't right. That isn't fair.

Farage hits back after Godfrey Bloom was ejected from the European Parliament for using Nazi language to describe German member Martin Schulz

Under the last leadership, at the 2010 election, we managed to produce a manifesto that was 486 pages long. You can quote me all sorts of bits from it I won't know, which is why I've said none of it stands today and we will launch it all after the European elections.

Farage finds himself hamstrung by some of UKIP's more eccentric policies in an interview with the BBC's Andrew Neil

I've never advocated that policy. If somebody in UKIP in the past did, well, so be it, but I think that people need to have a rounded education and sex education is part of that.

Farage seeks to disassociate himself from a policy, featured on the UKIP website, of not giving under-elevens sex education

The idea was it was election day. What do politicians do on election day? Well, normally they do very boring things. They go and visit a factory or visit a few polling stations. But I thought the idea of my hopping into a light aircraft and hooking up this banner and towing it round the constituency was a fun thing to do; it would make a good camera shot. I have been accused over the years of trying to pull off stunts – well, I suppose I'm guilty of that – and in this case it was a little bit the biter bit.

Farage speaks to the *Politics Show* on 16 May 2010 about his plane crash during the final day of the election that year

He started making drunken phone calls. I went to see him and he threatened to kill me. But for him to top himself like that, with a young kid and everything – not good.

Justin Adams, forty-eight, the pilot who flew Farage on his ill-fated election day flight, was found dead by police at his home. Mr Adams's wife left him after the crash, with the pilot accusing Farage of 'ruining his life'

Sadly he went completely crackers and started to believe his own publicity. And he didn't have the ability to laugh at himself, which is never a good thing in any walk of life.

Farage describing the behaviour of TV presenter Robert Kilroy-Silk, who was briefly a high-profile UKIP MEP. Despite Kilroy-Silk's bizarre behaviour in – and ultimate exodus from – UKIP, Farage still believes getting him to join was a 'mega catch' for the party

Politicians are smooth-talking sociopaths.

Godfrey Bloom on political leaders, presumably excluding himself and Farage

I had the most blistering row with Godfrey in a Strasbourg restaurant the other day.

Farage jokes about his relationship with controversial former UKIP MEP Godfrey Bloom during his speech to conference in 2013. Just hours later, Farage would have to defend the embattled MEP again, before Bloom eventually resigned

There are things that went wrong in his career. We all have things in our life that have gone wrong.

Farage defends his appointment of Neil Hamilton, the disgraced cash-for-questions former Tory minister, as UKIP's campaign manager

I do not find it acceptable that MEPs turn their backs on the European anthem or the flags of member states. I do not find shouting or rude remarks acceptable during plenary sessions, or that the majority of colleagues from Great Britain do not take part in the work of committees.

Iveta Grigule left Farage with a political headache in 2014 after ditching his EFDD group. The status of the group was saved by controversial Polish MEP Robert Jaroslaw Iwaszkiewicz

It is a vast sum ... I don't know what the total amount is but – oh Lord – it must be pushing £2 million...

Farage responds to a question from Denis MacShane – later disgraced himself – on his expenses and allowances as an MEP

I've been so busy this week I haven't yet had time to even sit down and write the speech that's going to happen at lunchtime. I'll work it out later.

Farage claims that his 2014 UKIP party conference speech was practically off-the-cuff

Tell them if they want a transcript of my speech they can fucking whistle for it.

Rod Liddle reveals a tired Farage swearing down the phone after journalists demanded copies of his 2014 conference speech, which Farage said he delivered without notes

I don't think I know anybody in politics as poor as we are.

Farage describes his financial situation, despite his MEP's salary and £540,000 house

SCOTLAND

Frankly, I've had enough of this interview. Goodbye.

Farage hangs up during a telephone interview with *Good Morning Scotland*. He was being questioned by David Millar following a turbulent visit to an Edinburgh pub, which ended with Farage being forced to flee protesters under police escort

I can quite understand a large number of Scottish voters viewing the career political class in Westminster with a degree of contempt. Please do not for one moment think of this as an entirely Scottish phenomenon.

Farage wades into the 2014 Scottish independence referendum and urges Scots to vote 'no', despite experiencing difficulties on previous visits north of the border

If this is the face of Scottish nationalism, it's a pretty ugly picture … The anger, the hatred, the shouting, the snarling, the swearing was all linked into a desire for the Union Jack to be burnt.

Farage describes the protesters who forced him to flee the Canons' Gait pub in Edinburgh

A student demonstration isn't the Dreyfus trial.

Alex Salmond responds to Farage's comments following the Canons' Gait pub incident

REFLECTIONS
OF A LEADER

I certainly have not been able to do what most dads do because of the pressures of the job. I have two grown-up sons and spent a bit more time with them in my old job. I have less time for the girls and that is a regret.

Farage on the pressures of being a high-profile leader and a father

This job is an unpaid job. It costs a fortune to do. You are on call seven days a week and all you get is aggravation.

Farage on being leader

If an idea is indeed sensible, it will eventually become just part of the accepted wisdom.

Farage, writing in *The Guardian*, describes how UKIP tax policy is apparently becoming the accepted wisdom

I believe we should have continued with the advance.

Despite suggesting it could have cost 100,000 more lives, Farage argued in an Armistice Day lecture last year that Britain and its allies should have continued fighting World War One for a further six weeks until they achieved Germany's unconditional surrender

[Their] priorities appear to be more concerned on the preservation of molluscs, beetles and water voles than our farmer and our householder; compliance with EU directives being more important than flood prevention.

Farage on the Environment Agency

[That] the British Olympic pistol team have to go to France to practise was just crackers.

Farage explains his position on bringing back 'properly licensed' handguns

It was selfie mania after my speech.

Farage gets down with the kids after giving a speech to A-level students

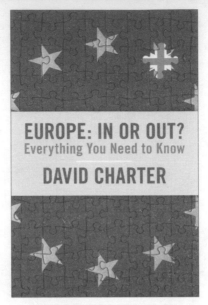